PORTSMOUTH
FROM THE AIR

including
Havant & Hayling,
Fareham, Gosport & Lee-on-the-Solent

Sunseekers crowding the beach on a hot summer day is not just a product of modern times, as this evocative picture of South Parade in the late 1930s proves. The only difference would be the ratio of bare flesh to costume, which is far greater in today's more relaxed atmosphere.

PORTSMOUTH
FROM THE AIR

including
Havant & Hayling,
Fareham, Gosport & Lee-on-the-Solent

Anthony Triggs

Phillimore

1995

Published by
PHILLIMORE & CO. LTD.
Shopwyke Manor Barn, Chichester, West Sussex

© Anthony Triggs, 1995

ISBN 1 86077 005 3

Printed and bound in Great Britain by
BIDDLES LTD.
Guildford, Surrey

For Sue and little Benny,
my travelling companions

Contents

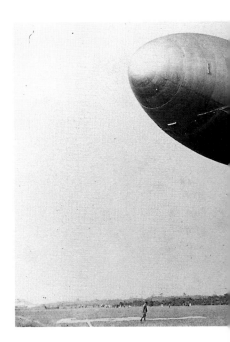

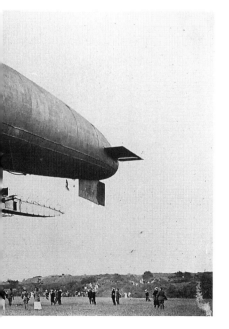

The airship 'Gamma' at Portsmouth in 1914

Acknowledgements

A great many people can become involved in compiling a book of this nature, and I would like to thank those who have taken both time and trouble to help, and I must start by thanking my publisher, Noel Osborne, and his staff for their support and encouragement.

Researching pictures is the biggest part of most local history writers' work, so my thanks must go to those individuals and organisations which have come to my aid.

Firstly I would like to thank Geoffrey Elliott, editor of *The News*, for permission to use pictures from the newspaper's collection.

Alan King and his most helpful colleagues at the Local Studies Department of Portsmouth Library; Sarah Quail, Portsmouth City Council Museums and Records Officer; Andrew Perry of the Post Office Archives, London; John Smith of Lens of Sutton; Lt Keith Howard of the HMS Sultan Museum; Jim Lapthorn; Keith Smith; and the Portchester Social Club.

And I must not forget my colleagues at *The News*, who are always so helpful and cheerfully put up with my queries. Thanks go to Brenda Jacob and the staff of the reference library, and to June Long and the members of the photographic department.

Finally there is a debt of gratitude which is always my greatest pleasure to acknowledge – that to my wife Sue, whose encouragement and help is ever present.

ANTHONY TRIGGS

Portchester, 1995

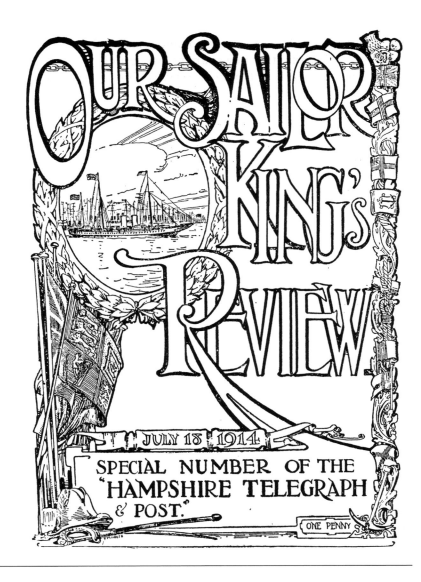

Chart of the Fleet for the
1914 Review.

8

Introduction

Nowadays aerial photography is commonplace. Whenever a big news story breaks the newspapers are quick to get their photographers into the air to provide readers with that all-important bird's eye view.

But at the dawn of the 20th century both photography and flight were in the very early stages, with satellite pictures and moon landings featuring only in the imaginations of fantasy writers.

The earliest known photograph was taken by the Frenchman Nicephore Niepce in about 1825, and after his death his work was carried on by his collaborator Louis Daguerre, whose 'daguerreotypes' involved capturing an image on a metal plate. The exposure times were measured in minutes – very often a neck clamp was used to hold a sitter – and there was no way of duplicating the image. Basically a daguerreotype was a one-off process.

In 1856 the French balloonist Felix Nadar used this process to take the first aerial picture – a view of Paris.

Meanwhile in England photography was progressing, and even before Nadar had taken his historic exposure a new process had been discovered by Londoner Frederick Scott Archer.

Archer had worked out that glass would be the best medium upon which to make a photographic image, but it had always been impossible to make the photographic emulsion adhere to it. In 1851 he discovered that a substance called collodion – gun cotton dissolved in ether – made a good binder, and as the glass plates could be made almost blemish free, the result was photographs of excellent quality.

However the system had two big drawbacks. Firstly the mixture had to be applied to the plate, exposed in the camera, and developed while still wet. This meant that the collodion photographer was forced to take his portable darkroom with him, usually contained in a purpose-built hand-cart. And secondly the exposure times were still uncomfortably long.

One exponent of this form of photography was Matthew Brady, who was commissioned to record the American Civil War. In September 1861 Brady took his camera aloft in the basket of the balloon Enterprise, which was tethered near the half-completed Capitol building in Washington. The slow speed of Brady's camera was no match for the movement of the balloon and consequently the resulting pictures were all but unusable. But the results did give President Lincoln, who attended personally, the idea that aerial photography had its uses – a fact that he built upon during the ensuing war years.

Among the official party watching the experiment was a young German nobleman, Count Ferdinand von Zeppelin, who later came to be linked with the rigid airships which were to bear his name.

As most early photography was directed towards use in war situations, in Britain the army took over aerial experiments, and in 1912 one of the pioneers of eye-in-the-sky photography, Sergeant A.V. Laws of the Royal Engineers and later of the Royal Flying Corps, made a breakthrough while flying in the dirigible airship Beta.

Because the early camera lenses distorted objects on the outer edges of photographs, more accuracy could be obtained by using only the centre sections. By taking photographs at intervals so that they overlapped, and using only the centre sections, a continuous strip of accurate photographs could be assembled.

But that technique held another great potential, as Laws was to discover.

Laws's photographs, when viewed through a stereo device, showed that, if the intervals between exposures were such that each showed 60 per cent of that covered by the previous one, then the images matched natural three-dimensional vision, giving depth to objects captured on the film. This process – photo-interpretation –

was used extensively during the Second World War to determine the positions of structures such as gun emplacements, which could not be accurately identified on normal flat pictures.

The slow speed of the airship enabled Laws to change his plates in the camera and still expose to the required intervals.

At the end of 1913 the decision was made to turn all army dirigible airship operations over to the Royal Navy. The four big balloons – Beta, Delta, Gamma, and Eta – along with experienced officers and men were transferred to the naval wing of the Royal Flying Corps.

Portmuthians had the opportunity to see the four giants of the skies in July the following year at the fleet review for George V, the sailor king. For the first time air power was represented at a review, and in addition to the airships a number of aircraft were on call.

With the threat of war looming, the purpose of the gathering was to test the fleet's readiness for battle. Various exercises were undertaken, one of which was to ascertain whether a German airship could actually bomb the dockyard. The Gamma, which had been moored at Fort Grange, Gosport, flew over the dockyard taking photographs and dropping dummy bombs.

Sadly, on review day, 18 July, the Gamma developed engine trouble and was forced to remain at Gosport for the duration.

By the eventual outbreak of war, the four airships were augmented by the Astra-Torres, bought from France. These five served throughout the war in what was by now the Royal Naval Air Service on anti-submarine patrols, convoy escort, and coastal photographic reconnaisance.

The Astra-Torres, a seven-ton monster, was used for patrols of about 12-hours duration over the Channel, and was the only British airship to be armed, carrying a Hotchkiss machine gun.

After the Great War, in which zeppelins featured very largely, the photographic techniques learned were used for more peaceful purposes, and the development of huge roll-film cameras put aerial photography into the leagues of an exact science, enabling exposures to be taken continuously, bearing in mind the faster speed of the aircraft carrying the equipment. The film used in these cameras were of an unconventional size – 5in to 9in wide – in 100-ft. rolls.

In 1932 another airship figured in the life of Portsmouth residents. On Saturday 4 July the municipal airport was opened by the under-secretary for air, Sir Philip Sassoon. There was a glittering display of flying, and a rumour that there was to be a visit from the pride of German airships, the Graf Zeppelin.

On 8 July 1928, on what would have been the late Count von Zeppelin's birthday, his only child, the Countess Hella von Brandenstein-Zeppelin christened the airship LZ127, the Graf Zeppelin. Thus began the eight-year career of the most famous of all airships.

The huge monster was 775 ft. long with a diameter of 100 ft., and was capable of a comfortable 70 miles an hour.

After the main show at Portsmouth, many members of the crowd stayed on, an intrepid reporter from the *Evening News* among

A rare Box Brownie shot of the huge Graf Zeppelin above the spectators at Portsmouth Airport.

them. When at 8.15 in the evening the giant of the skies arrived, he waxed lyrical in the edition of the following Monday.

'The coming of the Graf Zeppelin at the city of Portsmouth airport on Saturday evening made a fitting finish to what had been a great and important day.

'Although few could have known for certain that the Graf Zeppelin would pay the new airport a visit, large numbers of people remained after the programme had ended in the hope of seeing the wonderful airship which had set out from Germany that morning.

'A murmer of voices and some excited shouts at about 8.15 p.m. was the signal that something had been sighted in the north-eastern sky. Soon it was the all-absorbing object to which all eyes were directed.

'A mere speck. To the short-sighted it may have looked no more than a midge. It was not certain at first whether it was the expected Zepp, or just another aeroplane. But after a time there could be no doubting its identity. It was too compact to be an aeroplane: there were quite obviously no wings.

'Gradually, and really with surprising slowness, the blur became larger and larger and more definitely defined. And when it swung off the course laterally a little, a view of its length was obtained.

'The distant roar of its engines grew more persistent, and it was possible to discern the cars and the ribs of the superstructure. Nearer and nearer, until at last the huge leviathan of the skies hovered over the heads of the staring people below. Its name, Graf Zeppelin, was easily discernible.

'Leisurely, as if taking in the scene below, the airship glided over the field, gradually bearing off to the left.

'Waving arms from one of its cars drew an animated response from the spectators below. Hats were waved and voices cheered lustily. Possibly they cheered from the airship, but it was impossible to hear if they did.

'"Blimey! I didn't cheer the last one I saw," said a man to his friend. "Not likely!"'

However the euphoria was short-lived, for a week later, on 7 July, doubts were raised in Parliament over the wisdom of allowing the airship, and presumably its cameras, to fly over the city.

Sir Philip Sassoon replied to a question tabled by Sir Bertram Falle, Conservative MP for Portsmouth North. He stated that he was informed on reliable authority that the Graf Zeppelin, on its visit last Saturday, did not fly over any portions of the prohibited area of Portsmouth, and that no photographs were taken. Under the Anglo-German Air Agreement, he said, no formal permission for flight over any non-prohibited area was necessary.

Although the overview of Portsmouth did not alter a great deal during the '20s and '30s, pictures taken during that period serve to show how the city looked before the terrible battering of the Blitz. Between 1940 and 1944, 67 air raids dropped thousands of bombs on the city, most of the damage occurring in three attacks in August 1940, and January and March 1941.

In these attacks more than 500 people lost their lives, and a seven-hour raid on 10 January 1941 destroyed huge portions of the city, including Clarence Pier and the Hippodrome.

Altogether 930 civilians were killed and nearly 7,000 homes were destroyed in the aftermath of 38,000 incendiary bombs and 1,500 high-explosive bombs.

Sadly for some, 61 public houses and 49 beer houses were lost.

The Portsmouth skyline altered beyond recognition and, as the city regeneration took place it changed yet again, with high-rise building thrusting towards the sky.

And later, in the '70s, the construction of the motorway network brought even more expanses of roads into the city centre.

This collection of photographs aims to show the changes wrought over the landscape of Portsmouth and its surrounding areas over the period from 1914 to 1987, but from a different viewpoint.

The time covered is a relatively small number of years, but the pictures depict a lifetime of changes.

1 Portsmouth Dockyard

Because almost every naval vessel was at Spithead for the impending fleet review, the dockyard seemed deserted when the photographer aboard the airship Gamma took this picture on 15 July 1914.

However, in the distance, a train can be seen on the viaduct between the Harbour Station and the South Railway Jetty.

The area in the centre of the picture is the blackened site once occupied by the 1833 semaphore tower, which was destroyed on 20 December the previous year in a disastrous fire which claimed the lives of two watchmen.

The alarm was raised by a young employee of Chambers the fishmonger at Bonfire Corner, who had been making a delivery to the battle cruiser *Queen Mary* at the South Railway Jetty.

The blaze started in the sail and flag loft, which contained highly imflammable tarred ropes, signal flags and bunting, and within minutes it had spread to the interior beams of the tower.

The dockyard fire crews were soon at the scene, supported by the town fire brigade. Fire crews of 50 men each were mustered from the 15 warships in harbour, backed by teams from Fort Blockhouse, the Marines barracks at Eastney and at Forton, and the motor appliance from Clarence Barracks crossed the harbour on the floating bridge. Altogether more than 1,000 men fought the blaze, but to no avail.

With the threat of war with Germany looming, sabotage was suspected, but was never proved.

The Great War intervened, and the new tower was not completed until 1929, when the old Lion Gate (1777) – which had been demolished and put into store – was re-constructed at the base of the tower. The steel mast of the German cruiser *Nurnberg*, captured in the war, was placed at the top of the structure.

Facing page: The dockyard at Portsmouth is deserted as every ship of the line is anchored at Spithead for the royal review by George V on 18 July 1914.

Left: The newly-built semaphore tower, incorporating the old Lion Gate, is back in use in the dockyard.

2 Portsmouth Harbour

On the way from Fort Grange the airship Gamma passed over Gosport, and the astute cameraman took the opportunity to record the town for posterity.

High Street runs across the lower area of the picture, and in the harbour *Victory* is still afloat. At this time the venerable old vessel was a good money-spinner for the watermen, who offered trips giving visitors a close-up view.

The condition of *Victory* caused so much concern that in 1922 she was taken to her final resting place, in dry dock in the dockyard, where she underwent comprehensive restoration to bring her to the condition she was in at Trafalgar.

This move was a serious threat to the watermen, who had relied upon this little piece of tourism to supplement their income.

The Great War had ended, but the employment situation in the town was depressing. Great numbers of servicemen had returned to discover that little provision had been made for them. Because jobs were scarce, employers could exploit the position and keep wages low.

However, although the depression was looming, there was still some money to be made in the town. Camper and Nicholson's boatyard created the elegant yachts for the affluent racing community, providing employment for skilled labour and entertainment for local people on the launch days.

Sir Thomas Sopwith's *Endeavour* was launched in 1934, which proved to be such a spectacle that the boatyard was forced to issue tickets for vantage points. The later launches of *Endeavour II*, *Shamrock IV*, and *Shamrock V* were also big draws.

And to equip the yachts, Quay Lane was the home of one the greatest sailmaking firms, Ratsey and Lapthorn, which had been based in the town since 1790.

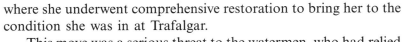

Facing page: The historic buildings of Gosport High Street were clearly recorded by the photographer aboard the airship Gamma in 1914.

Left: Work under way at Ratsey and Lapthorn's sail loft between the wars.

3 Southsea

In 1919 an observer aboard a Calshot-based seaplane took this picture of the area of Southsea that used to be known as 'Little India'.

Taking centre stage in the picture is St Bartholomew's Church, built in 1858 as the centrepiece of what was to be a new housing development with a retaining wall and four lodges.

The land had been bought by a Mr. Butcher, of Norwich, for £4,520. He called it Havelock Park as a tribute to the hero of the Indian Mutiny and, because other roads were named in a similar fashion – Outram, Campbell, and Lawrence – the area soon took on the soubriquet of Little India.

In any estate built in Victorian times a church was a necessity to encourage the 'right sort' of residents, and the first of these was a strange building, known because of its shape as the 'Crinoline Church'. It was of wooden construction with 20 sides and a roof which rose to a narrow apex, reminiscent of the garment.

By 1862, with the estate growing, a permanent church was built, and was dedicated to St Bartholomew, who was said to have evangelised parts of India. It was thought that this particular saint was chosen because of the 'Indian' identity of the estate.

The church was eventually demolished in 1958, and parts of the interior were transferred to St Matthew's, now the Church of the Holy Spirit. The oval-shaped area where the church once stood is now occupied by a small group of homes.

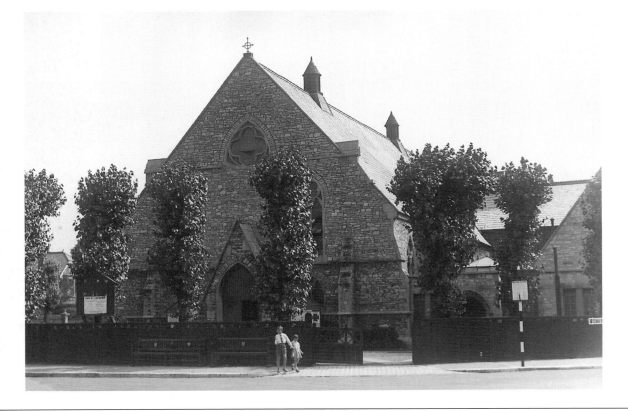

Facing page: St Bartholomew's Church shows up in the centre of this 1919 photograph.

Left: The church of St Bartholomew in Outram Road.

4 Southsea

Southsea owes its popularity mainly to the dockyard and to the services. Many naval officers and their families took to living or retiring in the area, and accordingly it gradually became known as a genteel place to live.

Southsea Common was owned by the government until 1923 when it passed into the hands of Portsmouth Corporation. Because the common was used for military purposes and defence, the seafront homes could only be built north of the open space, and not right on the front as in many other seaside towns.

Some of the common area was taken up by the Great Morass, which once extended northwards into what is now the Southsea shopping area.

During the late Victorian period Southsea began to take on the appearance of a neat seaside resort, and to add to its attractions. Clarence Pier was opened in 1861 with capital of £4,000. In 1874 the pier was enlarged to cater for an expected 4,000 visitors daily. South Parade Pier was opened in 1879 by Princess Edward of Saxe-Weimar, and was considered to be more fashionable than its smaller brother.

By the end of the century Southsea was a mature resort, and a guide of the time read: 'In this great conglomerate borough, Southsea may be regarded as the aristocratic section. Residences occupied by nobility and officers, as well as persons of wealth, are built in quality and quantity, a substantial proof of the excellence of the locale.'

Facing page: An early aviator taking a bird's-eye-view of Southsea. In the bottom of the picture is Lumps Fort, which was later sold to the corporation, and transformed into a rose garden and model village.

Left: A sadly-neglected Lumps Fort before Portsmouth took control.

5 Langstone

The twin land-based access routes to Hayling Island were the railway and the toll bridge.

The latter was opened in 1834 by the Duke of Norfolk and paid its way for many years. A century later, in 1938, a dispute arose over whether the bridge should be freed of charges. The members of the Waterloo and District Council said that if the people of Hayling could raise between £10,000 and £20,000 to replace the lost tolls, then the charge would be dropped.

Eventually, after further arguments between the council and other factions, the vote was taken that the toll was to stay.

Even when the new road bridge – which was the longest pre-stressed concrete bridge in the country at the time – was built in 1956, the toll continued, and it remained until 1960.

The earlier structure had a weight problem, and in the '50s it often meant that if more than a dozen or so passengers were aboard a bus about to cross, then the rest would have to get off and walk, and reboard when the bus reached the other side.

Facing page: A motor bus en route for Hayling is pictured passing the toll house in this view of the late '20s.

Left: A car makes its way over the toll bridge in the '30s.

6   Hilsea Ramparts

Portsmouth has been defended from the north since early times. It is thought that a bulwark was constructed on the northern side of Portsbridge in the reign of Henry VIII, but there was certainly a fort in existence during the Civil War.

In 1642 it was seized by Roundheads and its complement of eight were taken prisoner, and Portsea Island was taken.

As Britain became involved in various continental wars the Board of Ordnance directed that the fortifications of Portsmouth should be improved, and by 1757 the Hilsea Lines, a fortified line of bastions and retaining walls, was built on the northern shore of Portsea Island. It consisted of magazines, storehouses, and barracks for two battalions of foot soldiers.

Over the next 50 or so years the Lines were allowed to deteriorate, and not until the 1840s, when the government became aware of a very real threat from France, was thought put into the defences once more.

The Duke of Wellington wrote to the government commenting on the poor state of the country's defences, and in particular suggested it would be sensible to 'keep in repair the Lines of Hilsea'.

However by the 1850s, with the development of longer-range weapons, it was thought that a line of forts along Portsdown Hill was a better option, and Forts Nelson, Southwick, Widley, and Purbrook were built.

But the invasion never came, the Hilsea Lines became redundant, and by 1919 the Hilsea arches were demolished, followed later by the eastern bastion for the airport development.

Facing page: This view shows the northern part of the site proposed for the city airport before building commenced. These eastern parts of the ramparts were levelled and the moat in the picture filled in.

Left: Other sections of the ramparts were removed, and here workers are clearing the west bastion at Hilsea.

7   Southsea Common

The date is June 1931 and the four-day Royal Counties Agricultural Show has come to Southsea.

The show, which occupied 50 acres of the common and attracted more than 56,000 visitors, was first held in 1871 on the site of what is now Victoria Park. However the event was not without acrimony, as the enclosure of such a large area of common for the six months prior to the show led to a great public outcry.

The lord mayor, Councillor Walter Gleave, performed the opening ceremony on 3 June, and then proceeded to the site where the city airport was under construction and boarded a Gipsy Moth belonging to the Dominion Motor Spirit Company, from where he took a pleasure flight over the showground.

On the second day the show had a royal visitor when Prince George drove from London accompanied by Lady Louis Mountbatten.

He was entertained to lunch by the president of the Royal Counties Agricultural Society, Alderman Sir William Dupree, and later went on to tour the showground, taking special interest in the cattle parade and the four-in-hand driving contest.

There was also an exhibition by the National Hackney Society, when the crowd warmed to the colourful high-stepping horses in the ring.

More than 200 exhibitors set up on the site, with handicraft stands, bee-keeping displays, and parade of corporation horses.

Approximately £6,000 was offered as prize money, in addition to many cups and trophies, and exhibitors came from all areas of the country.

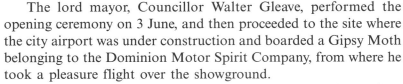

Facing page: The lines of marquees and show tents cover the common as the agricultural show takes up residence at Southsea.

Left: The common played host to later shows, and a prizewinner proudly displays his certificate and his champion animal at the event held in coronation year, 1953.

8 Old Portsmouth

Old Portsmouth can always be thought of as the birthplace of the greater city, for it was on this peninsula at the harbour mouth that the first settlement was made.

As time passed the tiny area became the focus of all seaborne activity, especially during the time of the Napoleonic wars.

Commercial shipping still uses the part of the harbour known as The Camber. Nowadays we think of a camber as a slope in a road, but earlier dictionaries also describe it as a place for the loading and unloading of sea vessels. Originally there was a bridge across the dock, but it was removed in 1924 to allow larger vessels to enter, leaving the *Bridge Tavern* as the only reminder.

The Old Portsmouth area was delineated by the fortifications and the old town gates, and beyond King James's gate – which stood near Sally Port – was the insular community called Point, or Spice Island.

In 1801, Motley's *History of Portsmouth* described it as: 'a place equally known and celebrated for its eccentricities in all parts of the world, where the navy or commerce of Great Britain has left of retained any vestiges.

'The street is filled with on of the most heterogenous assemblages of traffic and conviviality that is, perhaps, to be found in the same extent in any street, and in any part of the world.'

Facing page: Old Portsmouth with the cathedral taking pride of place. In the top right area can be seen the marquees of the agricultural show on Southsea Common (see previous page).

Left: The area of the Camber has changed over the years, and Dirty Corner – well-known before the war – has disappeared.

9 Portsmouth Airport

Portsmouth entered the air age in 1932 with the opening of the new airport, said by air ace Sir Alan Cobham to be 'the best aerodrome I have landed in'.

The scheme was first discussed by the city fathers in 1930, and three choices of location were suggested – Paulsgrove, Farlington, and an area known as Highgrove on the east of the city.

Highgrove, which was mostly farmland, was chosen, and altogether more than 76 acres were cleared, and 105,000 cubic metres of the old fortifications were blown up.

The airport opened on 2 July 1932, with a big display of flying, and an official ceremony by the under-secretary of state for air, Sir Philip Sassoon.

More than 110 planes took part in the air show, and the lord mayor and other civic dignitaries were given a joy ride in the Imperial Airways liner, *City of Liverpool*.

One of the first companies to set up operations was Portsmouth, Southsea, and Isle of Wight Aviation Ltd, which offered a regular service to the Isle of Wight. By June 1932 it had taken more than 1,000 people into the air, and the airport was not then officially open!

In subsequent years the airport played host to a number of air shows, and was the starting point for the ill-fated non-stop London-Karachi endurance bid by Sir Alan Cobham, when engine trouble caused the attempt to be abandoned at Malta.

After the war a regular service to the Channel Islands was started and ran successfully until 1967, when a double disaster sounded the death knell for the airport.

On 15 August, in torrential rain, a Hawker Siddeley 748 skidded on the slick grass runway while landing and ended up with its nose buried in an earth bank. To add to the problem, 90 minutes later a second 748 did the same, and crashed through the perimeter fence.

As a direct result the airport finally closed on 31 December 1973.

Facing page: A stunning view of the airport during a flying display, showing the line of enthusiastic spectators.

Left: Civic dignitaries are pictured waiting to board the *City of Liverpool* on the opening day of the airport.

10   Southsea

In the '30s Fawcett Road was a thriving shopping area, serving the thousands of workers who were part of a growing new culture.

THE **STATE**   PHONE 4244
CINEMA, FAWCETT ROAD, SOUTHSEA

GRAND OPENING PERFORMANCE TO-DAY, 3 p.m.

TO-DAY (SATURDAY), JULY 9th —— FOR FIVE DAYS

WILL HAY

IN

OH! MR. PORTER

Presented Daily at 3.25, 6.15, 9.5   (U.

Also JOHN LODER, ANNA LEE in "NON-STOP NEW YORK" (A)

ADMISSION—TWO PRICES ONLY.
Circle, 1/- . . . . Stalls, 6d.
SPECIAL BARGAIN MATINEES DAILY.
UP TILL 3.30 P.M.
Circle 6d. . . . Stalls 4d.

THURSDAY, JULY 14th —— FOR THREE DAYS

JACK BUCHANAN

IN

SMASH AND GRAB

Presented Daily at 3.35, 6.28, 9.21.   (U)
Also GEORGE ARLISS in " DOCTOR SYN " (A)

CONTINUOUS DAILY FROM 1.30 p.m.

The grid-iron straight rows of houses were built in the late Victorian years, when the earlier florid designs had changed to the simplified layout of long straight roads and streets.

In the bottom left of the picture is the beautiful Church of St Matthew, now the Church of the Holy Spirit.

The magnificent structure was the brainchild of the charismatic vicar, the Rev. Bruce Cornford, who purchased the plot of land for just under £900.

He appointed church designer John Thomas Micklethwaite as architect, and the result was a splendid place of worship seating a congregation of nearly two thousand. The church was consecrated in 1903.

Mr. Cornford died in 1940, and within a few months the church was hit by an incendiary bomb during the Blitz.

The outer shell remained, and now the totally gutted interior has been restored.

Two streets away can be seen the box-like structure of the local picture house. Opened in 1911 as the Southsea Electric, it was later renamed the Fawcett Picture House. By 1929 it had new owners and took on another new identity as The Capital, later changing again to The Commodore.

In 1938, after various alterations, it became The State, a name which only lasted a short while, as the cinema was closed in 1940.

After the war it became the Embassy Ballroom, but in the '60s social dancing became a casualty of television, and it closed for good. A block of flats, Embassy Court, now stands on the site.

Facing page: The orderly rows of streets in this picture show the late Victorian style of houses for the working population.

Left: An advertisement for the opening night at the State cinema, featuring a still-popular Will Hay film.

11   Hilsea, Portsmouth

Gas came to Portsmouth in 1821. The gasworks were built at Flathouse where there was easy berthing for colliers.

By 1875 increased storage capacity was needed, and a new gas holder was erected at Rudmore, with extra workshops and additional repair facilities.

Towards the end of the last century the new gasworks at Hilsea were laid out, and eventually were opened in 1904. The five million bricks needed were made on the site from the sub-soil of the estate.

Excavations beneath the main gas holder went down 40 ft., and in all nearly 40,000 cubic yards of material was removed.

The company amalgamated with Havant and Emsworth in about 1925, and when the Gosport company was absorbed in 1936 the company name was changed to the Portsmouth and Gosport Gas Company. The Hayling Island Gas Company was taken over in 1937.

By 1938 there were 1,400 employees, and the company boasted the best staff care available, with a pension fund, life insurance, and a sickness benefit scheme.

Facing page: The sprawl of the gas company's premises with its then ultra-modern equipment is already being encroached upon by residential housing.

Left: Production is under way in the Hilsea gasworks.

12   North End, Portsmouth

On 7 October 1932, Portsmouth made a very real effort towards the solution of a serious post-war problem – an ever-increasing demand for education – with the opening of the new Northern Secondary School in Mayfield Road – now the Mayfield School.

Previously the boys' school had been operating in temporary accommodation for 11 years, and there had been no proper educational facilities for girls in the northern part of the city.

The opening ceremony was performed by the Lord Mayor of Portsmouth, Alderman Ferdinand Foster, before an invited – if tightly packed – audience of 500 adults and 200 pupils.

The nine-acre site had been bought from Winchester College, and the total cost, including furniture, was £125,000, and the school provided places for 570 boys and the same number of girls.

For its time the building had every modern convenience. In addition to the 36 classrooms there were two libraries, two gyms, two lecture theatres, four art rooms, and nine science labs. For a healthy diet there were two dining halls with kitchens attached, and for bodily health the school boasted two playing fields – one for boys and the other for the girls.

At the ceremony the architect, Adrian Sharp, said the health of pupils was as important as education in the design of the school. Classrooms were arranged to get maximum sunlight and fresh air, and each classroom was cross ventilated.

The design was considered to be so up-to-date that for a week before the opening the building was available for inspection, with regular tours for interested parents.

Facing page: The school, with the twin playing fields, stands out among the lines of housing at North End.

Left: A closer look at the front elevation of the advanced school.

13 Havant

At the bottom of the picture the railway line to Hayling Island can clearly be seen. The line was officially opened in 1865, although at that time it only ran as far as Langstone.

Eventually, after a few initial delays, the first train ran on 17 July 1867, the second day of the Hayling Races.

The Hayling Bridge and Causeway Company ran the line until 1922, when it was absorbed into the great maw of the Southern Railway. Because of the weak bridge only small engines were used, but usage took its toll and by 1966 £400,000 was needed to effect repairs to the bridge. The work was never done, and eventually the last train ran on 2 November 1963, the end of an era.

In its time the line carried thousands of passengers to the holiday isle, and the Terrier engines, of only 28 tons, were considered to be 'quaint' and therefore added to the appeal of the journey.

Sometimes in the summer months an extra 'pram' van was added to carry holidaymakers' baby carriages.

All that is left of such a popular undertaking is the old goods shed and the stumps of the bridge trestles.

Facing page: The Hayling Billy railway line can be seen at the bottom of the picture. Now the line of the track is a popular walk.

Left: The other way to reach Hayling was the ferry from Eastney, here pictured in the '30s.

14 East Southsea

Residents and visitors take the bracing air on a sunny Southsea afternoon.

A popular place to sit and watch the Solent traffic was – and still is – the continuous sea wall seat.

At this end of the beach there was always a problem of high winds blowing shingle into the roadway, and it was borough engineer Percy Boulnois who built the wall, which to a large degree alleviated the situation.

Boulnois held his position from 1883 to 1900, and in his time left several important marks upon the layout of Portsmouth.

To the north of the road is the Royal Marines Barracks, which were built during a period from 1862 to 1867. Before that the corps had been based at Fort Blockhouse.

The great water tower was a later addition to the original construction, and was built in 1871 to feed the fire mains. The clocks were added later still, and were brought from Woolwich dockyard.

Eastney barracks received a noble visitor in 1890, Germany's Kaiser Wilhelm. He inspected the troops and remarked, somewhat prophetically: 'I consider the British Royal Marine is the best all-round fighting man in the world'.

Later, during the Great War, the marines from Eastney served on the Western Front with outstanding gallantry.

Facing page: Sunseekers crowd the beach with the line of brand-new beach huts behind them.

Left: Holidaymakers relax on the sea wall seat, while a few motorists take to the seafront.

15 Milton, Portsmouth

Milton has always been thought of as the last of the villages of Portsea Island.

Its old cottages and forge lasted into the 20th century, and even in the 1920s it was a popular Sunday afternoon destination for Portsmouth folk who wished to sample a piece of rural life.

However Locksway Road, once named Hospital Lane, tells the story of a venture that failed – the Portsmouth-Arundel canal. Once the canal could have been traced from its basin in Portsmouth – Arundel Street was named with the waterway's eventual destination in mind – along Canal Walk, and through Milton where the remains of the lock gates still stand.

The canal was opened in 1823 with great optimism. The ambitious scheme planned to link Portsmouth with London, by way of the Thames, Wey, and Wey and Arun Canal. It was hoped to connect the capital with the great French ports through the most advantageous outlet.

However it was doomed to failure because of two basic reasons. Firstly, the sea water in the waterway seeped into the water supplies of neighbouring houses and polluted it, and secondly, the railways were overtaking water as a cheap method of transport.

By 1832 the canal was drained and when the railways eventually came to Portsmouth, part of the canal bed near Fratton Bridge was used as a cutting.

Facing page: Milton foreshore, clearly showing the long line of the defunct canal from its seaward entrance.

Left: A walk by the sea in the balmy days before modern development had changed the coastline.

16 Fratton, Portsmouth – 1930

Fratton Park, the home of Portsmouth Football Club, dominates this picture. Milton Road is in the foreground, and Velder Avenue runs out of the picture at the bottom.

Pompey was formed in 1898, as a result of Southampton Football Club's success after turning professional.

In April 1898 a syndicate of six businessmen and sportsmen met in Old Portsmouth and resolved to buy a parcel of agricultural land near Goldsmith Avenue, with the intention of building a football pitch.

The land cost nearly £5,000, and in September of the same year the club chairman, local brewery magnate Sir John Brickwood, announced at a special meeting of shareholders that it was hoped that the pitch would be playable for the 1899-1900 season.

However, it is amusing to note that the ground had yielded a huge crop of potatoes, which the club was eager to sell.

Things moved on, the ground was levelled and turfed and a 100 ft. stand was constructed on the south side, with a 240 ft. one on the north.

Eventually the directors were told that the park had cost £6,538 with the stands, dressing rooms and turnstiles costing a further £9,372.

It was also noted that the players' wages were to be £4 a week.

Facing page: Fratton Park with Fratton railway station in the background, with the long curve of the East Southsea line going out of the picture to the left.

Left: An early Pompey team taken by local photographer Steven Cribb, who was also a later chairman of the club. Cribb followed the progress of his team until his death in 1963.

17 Stokes Bay, Gosport – 1935

The importance of Stokes Bay as a defensive position became apparent in the 16th century when Henry VIII built Haselworth Castle.

It is first mentioned in 1545, but seems to have had a short life. In 1669 the Earl of Warwick built two sea markers, to guide ships into the safe water passage of the harbour. They were built of stone, and were still considered of great importance in the 18th century for they were heightened on brick piers.

One was known as the Kicker-Gill, and the other the Gill-Kicker. Gradually the name became shortened to Gilkicker. The Kicker-Gill was pulled down as late as 1965.

Along the coast to the west still stands Bay House – a Victorian seaside residence.

It was built in 1838 for Alexander Baring, the first Baron Ashburton, an eminent politician and financier. The building was designed by Decimus Burton – who built the Athenaeum club in London – and was constructed mainly of French stone from Caen. It became a focus for entertaining royalty and politicians.

In 1870 the building was sold to the Rev. Edward Burney who established a naval college, and in 1892 it passed to Col. Francis Sloane-Stanley.

Sloane-Stanley was a keen yachtsman, and the family were close friends with Edward VII, and it is reputed that the king used to slip over to the relaxing Bay House from the restrictive atmosphere of Osborne.

After the war Bay House became an overflow building for the Gosport County Grammar School, and today is part of the Bay House School complex, blending its old Victorian splendour with modern educational architecture.

Facing page: Stokes Bay, and the pier which was the terminus for the Stokes Bay railway line. Fort Gilkicker is in the foreground.

Left: A summer's day on the lawns of the Victorian Bay House.

18   Southsea Common

The brand-new bandstand sits on the common, soon to become a popular venue for late-night open-air dances in the summer evenings of the '30s.

The bandstand was later converted to encompass the roller-skating craze, and then in the '80s it took on the additional rôle of skateboard track.

In the background can be seen the Royal Naval War Memorial, which was erected to commemorate the 9,700 officers and men of the Portsmouth Port Division who lost their lives at sea in the Great War and have no burial place.

The Portsmouth memorial was one of three, identical in design, which were raised by the Imperial War Graves Commission. The other two were at Chatham and Plymouth, and were designed by Sir Robert Lorimer who was present at the dedication ceremony.

On 15 October 1924, the Duke of York unveiled the imposing structure after inspecting a guard of honour of 100 men and three officers from HMS *Vernon*.

It was estimated that between 25,000 and 30,000 spectators gathered on the common to watch the ceremony.

The memorial joins others along Clarence Esplanade, all of which recall historic naval actions.

Facing page: The bandstand. with its white wooden construction, stands out on the Southsea Common.

Left: With the war memorial in the background, sightseers at Clarence Esplanade watch the aircraft carrier USS *Randolph* enter harbour on 9 July 1947. The huge vessel, along with the battleships New Jersey and Wisconsin, was paying a 10-day visit to Portsmouth.

19   Copnor, Portsmouth – 1933

Copnor is mentioned in Domesday Book with the description: 'Robert, the son of Gerold, holds Copenore, and Heldred holds it under him, and Tovi held it under Earl Godwin'.

In the reign of Elizabeth I, the manor of Copnor with Portsea was in the possession of Henry, Earl of Southampton. It is likely then that Copnor and Portsea were formerly part of the possessions of Titchfield Abbey.

Copnor Lane was an ancient trackway which ran between Kingston and Copnor, roughly where Powerscourt Road and Queens Road are now situated.

At the time of the Great War there was just a handful of roads around the Baffins Pond area, with nothing to be seen northwards except Great Salterns Farm.

Salt production along the coast had probably been in operation since Roman times. In 1666 the Great Salterns were established. The pans produced salt for the navy victualling department, and by the 17th century the Portsmouth-produced material was considered to be the best in the country.

Facing page: Copnor Road runs diagonally across the picture, with the new Northern Secondary School in the background.

Left: Copnor Bridge, opened in 1908, already well in use by various forms of transport.

20 Hilsea, Portsmouth – 1934

Much of the Hilsea area consisted of land owned by the War Office. However early in the century, with the French invasion threat diminished, much of it was disposed of for development.

The old Portsbridge was replaced in 1927, and although new road developments have overtaken this, the eastern side of the bridge with its commemorative plaque can still be seen in the car parking area.

The Hilsea Lines were pierced and huge amounts of the old fortifications were demolished to make way for the Southdown bus company garage, which still stands today, albeit under a new guise.

The eastern end of the Lines became Hilsea Lido, which was opened in 1935, and the east demi-bastion became the changing rooms for the Portsmouth Grammar School playing fields.

North of the water the 'clearance land', which was kept free of buildings to allow the guns to sweep across Port Creek, was sold off, and during the years 1933-34 the Highbury estate was built. The smart homes with all modern conveniences went on the market from £595, a far cry from today's inflated values.

In 1931 the old *Coach and Horses* public house was demolished, and a new hostelry was built on the site.

The original inn, and acres of land around it, had been acquired by the government in 1858 to build the Hilsea Lines. Since then the inn had been leased from the War Office by Sir William Dupree. When it was decided to sell off the land, he was asked £10,000 for the freehold – in those days a great deal of money. His annoyance was such that he commissioned an enormous painting to be hung on the outside wall of the building showing a stagecoach being held up, with a poetic caption likening the highwayman to Asquith, then Chancellor of the Exchequer.

The picture, which was reproduced in painted tiles on the rebuilt inn, can still be seen.

Facing page: The Highbury estate is bottom left, with the small area used by the building company to off-load materials, much of which was brought in by water, along Port Creek.

Left: The old *Coach and Horses* public house. Note the original painting on the wall, and the Foden steam lorry on the forecourt.

21 Alverstoke, Gosport

The Stokes Bay rail line is recalled in this picture, with the track bed running diagonally from the bottom.

With Queen Victoria's preference for the Isle of Wight, it was thought the island would become more popular with the ordinary holidaymaker, and Stokes Bay seemed an ideal stepping-off place.

The Stokes Bay Railway and Pier Company was formed in 1855 with capital of £24,000. It was eventually opened in 1863 after a series of delays, which also pushed up considerably the cash requirements.

The line measured nearly two miles, and ran from the Gosport station to Stokes Bay pier. On its way it passed a new halt – Stoke Road station – later renamed Gosport Road station, which stood near the *White Hart* public house.

In the picture the station and its footbridge can be seen just north of the creek. Above it the line curves up towards the triangle junction and makes its way to Gosport station, out of the picture to the right.

In its final years the line was only used in the summer, as winds prevented the steamers from mooring at the pier. The last train ran in 1915, the line was closed, and the pier and track were bought by the Admiralty.

Facing page: The cluster of buildings comprising the Gosport House of Industry can be seen at the appropriately named Workhouse Creek, just above the white oval of the sports track.

Left: A lone rail employee on the platform of the Gosport Road station in the 1930s after traffic had ceased.

22 The Solent

The British Empire rejoiced on 6 May 1935, when George V and Queen Mary celebrated their silver jubilee – commemorating 25 years on the throne.

The weather seemed to celebrate as well, for on the day it was so hot that many people fainted from the heat.

A huge thanksgiving service was held in the Guildhall Square, and in the evening more than one hundred trams and buses conveyed revellers to the summit of Portsdown Hill to watch the highlight of the day, when the lord mayor, Councillor Frank Privett, lit a beacon to continue the chain running all around the coastline.

Two months later, on 15 July, the King, accompanied by the Prince of Wales and the Dukes of York and Kent, arrived at Cosham railway station. The royal party had come to Portsmouth for the jubilee review of the fleet at Spithead.

Dense crowds cheered the King on his five-mile journey to the dockyard.

The next day he reviewed the assembled fleet – a line of ships stretching for 27 miles – and in the evening crowds on the mainland were treated to a fireworks and searchlight display from the illuminated vessels.

The King left on the following day. It was the last time the people of Portsmouth were to see their monarch, as he was to die on 20 January the next year.

Facing page: The mighty fleet at Spithead, at anchor for the review by George V.

Left: The royal party is greeted upon arrival at Cosham railway station.

23 Fort Rowner, Gosport

The massive forts of Rowner and Grange were a solid backdrop to an airfield that earned a special place in the history of flight.

Sited west of the forts, the old Grange airfield has now all but disappeared beneath the later development of HMS *Sultan*.

Flying started in 1909 when Portsmouth Aero Club set up its headquarters at Fort Monckton, overlooking the Solent.

In 1910 the War Department gave the club permission to transfer activities to Grange.

A few years later a most remarkable aviator, Robert Smith Barry, developed at Gosport his revolutionary method of training pilots for combat. After service with the British Expeditionary Force in France he returned to Grange, and while there he developed a new communication system between pilot and instructor. Forever known as the Gosport Tube, the equipment stayed in service until the end of the Second World War.

With the formation of the Fleet Air Arm in 1924, the squadrons expanded, and by the '30s both RAF and navy personnel worked together under the growing threat of war.

When hostilities eventually started the base became a hive of industry with army searchlight units installed.

Grange had been under RAF control since 1922, but on 1 August 1945 it was brought under naval jurisdiction, and became HMS *Siskin*. In 1956 HMS *Sultan* moved from Portsmouth, and the base became the largest mechanical training establishment.

Facing page: The unusual stubby shape of a Blackburn Dart aircraft makes a novel foreground for Fort Rowner below.

Left: Lindbergh's *Spirit of St Louis* at Gosport in 1927 from where it was crated and taken by road to Southampton to be loaded aboard a transatlantic liner for the journey home to the United States. The aircraft can now be seen in the Air and Space Museum in Washington DC.

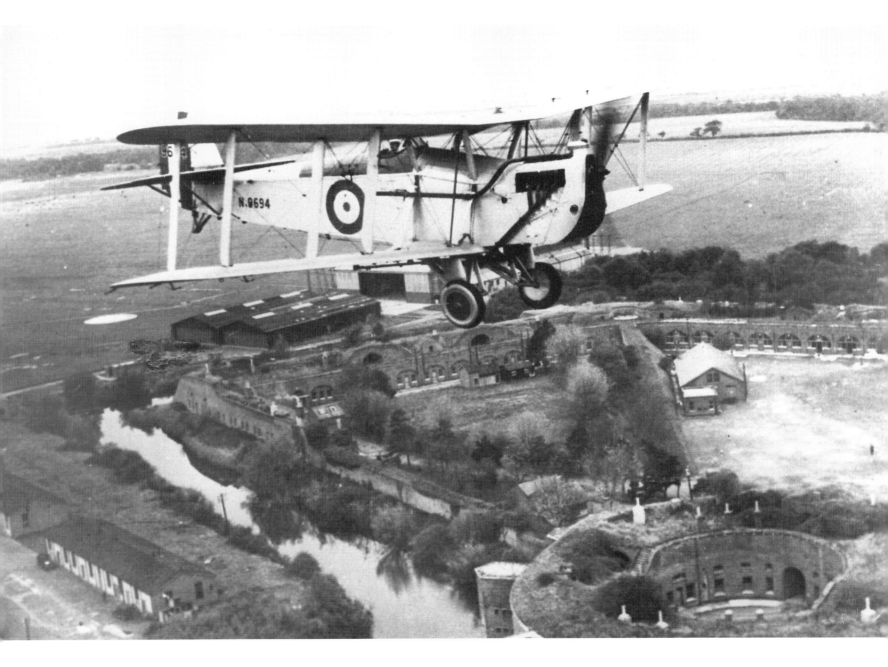

24 Lee-on-the-Solent

The tiny hamlet of Lee-on-the-Solent first came to prominence in the late 19th century, largely because of the efforts of local landowner Sir John Robinson, who had plans to turn it into a watering place of the best quality.

The highlight of the resort's layout was the Marine Parade, 50-ft. wide and a mile in length, providing between it and the sea a wide expanse of grassland running to the cliff edge.

Other plans included a pier, and a railway.

The railway line came to Lee in 1894, with a three-mile track from the main line at Fort Brockhurst, Gosport, via Gomer Halt and Browndown.

At first the line was operated by an independent company, but came under the jurisdiction of the Southern Railway in 1923. The new owners looked at the accounts and running costs of the line, and decided there and then to close it down.

They finally succeeded in 1930 as far as passengers were concerned, while goods traffic continued for a few years more.

The terminus building still stands, although now it does duty as an amusement arcade.

But the biggest white elephant of the town was assuredly the Lee Tower complex, with its cinema, restaurant, dance hall, and 120-ft. high tower. It was opened in 1935, but by 1937 the company went into liquidation. The tower survived the war, and in those post-war years only the cinema remained open. The tower complex itself was finally demolished in the '60s.

Facing page: The Lee Tower complex takes shape on the shoreline, a hope for the future, but destined to dominate the skyline for only 35 years. The short-lived railway line can be seen to the right of the picture.

Left: The tower in the '50s after many of its attractions had closed, leaving only the cinema to keep the dream alive.

25 South Parade Pier, Southsea

The crowded beach at South Parade clearly evokes a summer's day in the '30s.

The pier had always been a popular destination for visitors, and as early as 1928 it was recorded that during the months of July, August and September 733,478 people visited it. And for those seeking a sea trip, boat passengers from the pier numbered 263,160 for the same period.

When the pier reopened in 1909 after the disastrous fire of 1904, the first year's revenue was £8,000, but by the early '30s it was bringing in excess of £40,000 into the city coffers.

Out to the right of the picture is the Canoe Lake, which at one time boasted a popular swannery, and beyond that is Cumberland House.

The site of the house was unique in that it was the only dwelling between the Marine Drive and the sea. Many residents were concerned that it would be used for commercial purposes, as a company wanted to acquire it for a petrol filling station. However their fears were allayed when it was bought for the city and converted into an art gallery and museum, a role which it still fulfills today.

Facing page: Holidaymakers can be seen taking the air on the pier as a pleasure craft makes its way towards the landing stage.

Left: Cumberland House as it was when it was purchased to enhance the cultural attractions of the city.

26   Clarence Parade, Southsea

In 1922, when Southsea Common was sold by the War Department to Portsmouth, the council decided to spend £60,000 to convert it to gardens and playgrounds.

Provision was made for grass and hard tennis courts, a bowling green, putting green, and football and lacrosse pitches. The gardens and the Ladies' Mile were developed during the winter of 1924-25.

By 1929 land at the west of Southsea Castle was given over to a children's area with a paddling pool, boating lake, and a miniature railway, together with swings and a sand pit. To make it more attractive to visitors the road along the front to Clarence Pier was remade.

To lend more weight to their optimism, the council produced a guide book which included a 40-inch coloured panorama of Portsmouth by the celebrated Old Portsmouth marine artist W.L. Wyllie. The success of this can be measured, for in 1929 alone 33,000 copies were distributed worldwide to inquirers.

More than 9,000 coloured lights were festooned from Clarence Pier to South Parade Pier to add to the holiday atmosphere and to encourage familes with children to visit the resort.

Facing page: Thomas Ellis Owen's St Jude's Church stands out from the tightly-packed shops and houses, while sunseekers enjoy the attractions of Southsea.

Left: The Southsea miniature railway carries its young passengers on a voyage of fun.

27 Havant

That great traveller and writer, Arthur Mee, described Havant in the Hampshire volume of his *King's England* series.

'Havant,' he wrote, 'has lost one of the most interesting little trades in England, which was carried on here for about a thousand years.

'We found sheepskins hanging here in one of the little streets, outside the place where it was turned into some of the best parchment in the world.'

Mee pondered that precious documents on parchment made in the town could have ended up in strong rooms, parliaments and palaces everywhere. In fact, Havant parchment was considered to be the best in the world because of its whiteness, compared with others which had a yellow tinge. This, apparently, was a by-product of the water from the Homewell spring, from which, indirectly, Havant derives its name.

The industry finally ceased in 1936 when the last yard, Stallards, closed, leaving only Homewell, Potash Terrace, and The Parchment to remember it by.

The parchment was made from the inner layer of sheepskin, and the outer layer provided raw material for another business – glove making. Obviously gloves were worn long after parchment ceased to be commonly used, and this little industry continued until the '60s.

Facing page: The wide open spaces of Havant are clear on this picture taken in the late '30s. The railway station is in the middle of the view, with North Street running down the picture to St Faith's Church.

Left: Parchment making was big business in Havant, but here all that is left are the redundant pits.

28   Wymering, Portsmouth – 1933

Nowadays the foreshore area of Wymering and Paulsgrove could be considered built-up, but before the war it was a popular venue for the racing fraternity.

On 10 August 1928, Portsmouth Racecourse opened. The brainchild of local businessman George Cooper, who lived at nearby Paulsgrove House, it measured seven and a half furlongs, and boasted accommodation for 8,000 punters, with luncheon bars, a restaurant, and parking spaces for more than 2,000 cars.

The members' clubhouse was luxurious, expensively furnished with a private bar and a balcony from where the fortunate few could watch the racing.

In the construction more than 40,000 square yards of turf was removed from the slopes of Portsdown Hill, and when the track was finished it was considered to be second to none in the country. Torrential rain during the weeks preceding the opening helped to knit the turfs together to form a superb surface.

Finally, to accommodate to influx of racegoers, a railway halt was built at Wymering.

Facing page: The long oval of the racetrack stands out on the open fields, with the railway line and the bridge clearly visible.

Left: The final stage of the five-furlong Formby Handicap on 5 September 1932. The race was won by Royal Double.

29 Leigh Park

In the early '40s it became increasingly obvious to Portsmouth Council that an out-of-town overspill area was needed for housing.

The plan to obtain some 2,400 acres of land at Leigh Park was born in October 1943 when Councillor Frederick Storey proceeded with negotiations. Leigh Park House and adjoining land totalling 497 acres was initially purchased, followed by a further 1,174 acres. By 1947 negotiations to buy another 792 acres were under way.

The estimated population of the estate was between 21,000 and 25,000, with 6,000 to 7,000 homes planned, and at the time it was emphasised that architectural control was of paramount importance because of the natural beauty of the site. However in the years that followed, the harsh realities of housing need and financial deprivation altered the original image almost beyond recognition.

The first turf was cut by the lord mayor, Councillor Frank Miles, on 15 September 1947.

During the war Leigh Park House was home to the Royal Naval mines design experts, who officially vacated the building in 1956. Eventually, by 1958, it was demolished, a decision regretted in later years.

Facing page: Leigh Park in its early days, with just a few roads laid out, presenting a very different aspect to the estate of today.

Left: Skaters take to the ice on the lake in the grounds of Leigh Park House in the cold winter of 1927-28. In the background is the imposing house which was the main building on the beautiful estate.

30 Eastern Road, Portsmouth

In the late '20s it became apparent that increasing traffic would need improved access to Portsea Island from the mainland, so by 1927 the new widened Portsbridge was opened.

However it had long been a dream to open a second route on the eastern side of the island, and in 1928 that dream neared reality when the roads and works committee agreed the Eastern Road scheme.

The road was to run from Copnor, across the Farlington Marshes to Fir Tree Corner at the foot of Bedhampton Hill, but this route was changed so that the road would meet the Havant Road at Farlington.

The first section was completed, but it soon became known as 'The Road to Nowhere', leading only to the golf course and the city airport, then still known as the municipal aerodrome. It cost £86,000, half of which was paid by the government.

It was hoped the continuation would provide much-needed work for the many jobless, but high unemployment and spending cuts often run hand-in-hand, and the plan was put on ice until 1934, when the second section was completed, taking the road as far as Port Creek.

The bridge was completed by 1938, by 1941 the road was open to traffic, and the following year it was officially opened by the lord mayor, Sir Denis Daley, fullfilling a great need for the city.

Facing page: Eastern Road, dubbed the 'Road to Nowhere', leading only to the municipal aerodrome.

Left: The Roads and Works Committee members inspect the partly-completed Eastern Road.

31 Commercial Road, Portsmouth

A rain of German bombs in 1941 spelled the end of a Portsmouth tradition when the premises of the Landport Drapery Bazaar were destroyed. Instead of the popular store there was just a huge scar on the already ravaged landscape of the city.

Landport's had begun as a small drapery business in 1870, and as the years progressed it became a city institution. The store had survived a fire in 1910, and had used the disaster to rise again and provide even more services for its customers.

But the Blitz was too much, and overnight the showplace of Portsmouth shopping had vanished. Gone were the sweeping staircase, the ornate fixtures, and the restaurant where an orchestra played while four-course lunches were served for 1s. 6d. (7.5p).

But on 26 April 1954 – to the acclaim of one of the biggest crowds Commercial Road had ever seen – the newly rebuilt store was opened.

In 1965 the store was bought by the United Drapery Group, and in 1974 a huge refurbishment programme was completed. And on 3 May 1982 it changed its name to Allders – the trading name of the group – and with the name change came another extension, making it the store we know today.

Facing page: The site is cleared and building work starts on the new post-war store, to replace the one lost in the Blitz.

Left: A later Landport's, in the days when a policeman could still be seen on point duty at busy junctions.

32   Lee-on-the-Solent

For a small seaside resort, Lee-on-the-Solent's pier was quite a structure. It was 750 ft. in length, longer than South Parade Pier at Southsea, which was only 600 ft. from mainland to end.

For the first 200 yards it was only 15 ft. wide, although this spread to 34 ft. for the remainder.

For a short boat crossing to the Isle of Wight, the pier was ideal and after the opening ceremony on 3 April 1888 the steamer *Princess*

Beatrice arrived with a full complement of passengers.

Concert parties were a popular attraction too, and talent shows drew audiences from much of the area. In 1911 the young Noel Coward made his stage debut in one such show at Lee.

However on 19 June 1932, tragedy struck the pier when an electrical fault caused a spark which ignited the timbers of part of the superstructure, and within minutes the pier was ablaze. Despite the efforts of both the Gosport fire brigade and a detachment of service firefighters from the nearby air base, the fairy palace at the end of the pier was destroyed, with damage estimated at £35,000.

After that the pier never regained its former popularity, and a few years later on the outbreak of war the War Office sounded its death knell when it breached part of the landward area to prevent the structure being used by the enemy as a landing point.

Facing page: Lee pier in the post-war years. The stark girders of the seaward end are all that is left.

Left: The aftermath of the blaze, and firemen damp down the wreckage of the pier. A radiator stands like a piece of strange modern art amongst the embers.

33   Portchester

For centuries Portchester was just a small group of homes clustered around the historic castle. However this all changed at the time of the Napoleonic Wars when up to 8,000 French prisoners were held in the castle. This necessitated nearly 3,000 troops to guard them, and as a result the number of taverns, inns, and other quarters expanded northwards up what is now Castle Street.

In the 1850s, when the railway arrived, the village expanded northwards yet again, and Station Road and Hill Road today follow the ancient trackway over the hill to Southwick.

The village was self-sufficient, with a bakery and two windmills providing the flour. The stump of one mill still stands in private grounds along the foreshore near the castle. The other – more westward and known as the Wicor Mill – was demolished around 1920, and the site was used by a factory until fairly recently, when it too closed to be followed by a housing estate.

Cornaway Lane still runs from the Wicor area to the main Fareham-Portsmouth road, and in the past the name must have had a very literal meaning.

Facing page: A superb view of the crossroads at Portchester before the village shopping area was made into a precinct. Station Road runs northwards, and the railway bridge at the station can be seen in the top left-hand corner.

Left: West Street after the war, when traffic – although much less than today – between Portsmouth and Fareham would have passed through the village.

34 Spithead

All eyes were directed towards the Solent on 15 June 1953 for the huge fleet review to celebrate the coronation of Queen Elizabeth II.

The new monarch, aboard the frigate-yacht HMS *Surprise*, sailed proudly out of Portsmouth harbour to pass along the great lines of seaborne power.

The Queen had come to the city the evening before, and her car was so slowed down by the enormous crowds of wellwishers that she was 40 minutes late arriving at the dockyard. She was already behind time because of similar shows of affection in the towns and villages on her route from Windsor.

It was estimated that there were more than 20,000 cars and buses in Portsmouth as visitors descended on the city to join in the celebrations.

Special trains had been laid on to bring all the MPs, peers, and Commonwealth representatives to the city. At Portsmouth Harbour station a shuttle service of British Railways steamers took the guests out to HMS *Perseus* to see the Queen's progress through the fleet, the turning point of which was Horse Sands Fort, where the mighty *Vanguard* was moored.

Facing page: The great liner *Queen Elizabeth*, outward bound, passes through the ranks of ships moored ready for the review.

Left: Leave it to the navy! The main gate at Gunwharf decorated to celebrate the coronation.

35 Gosport

The Ferry Gardens, opened in 1925, and now the Falklands Gardens, whose symmtrical pattern shows up on this view of the busy harbour.

A ferry leaves a wake as it turns in its approach to the Gosport landing stage, where the ringing of the bell warned thousands of workers of the vessel's imminent departure.

Next to the landing stage the chain ferry – or floating bridge – is just leaving for Portsmouth. These huge craft started operations in 1840 and provided a way of getting horses, cattle, and larger vehicles across the harbour with relative ease.

The company ran four patriotically named vessels – the *Victoria*, *Albert*, *Alexandra*, and *Duchess of York* – and, because the ferries ran on chains, they could cross the harbour even in foggy conditions when the ordinary passenger ferries were stopped.

However in the '50s and '60s wages and costs took their toll and the company ran into financial difficulties. The *Duchess* had been grounded, and by 1959 both the *Duchess* and *Alexandra* were so badly in need of repairs that more than £20,000 was required to put them right.

The cash was never forthcoming, and the company ceased operations in December of that year, ending more than a century of service.

Facing page: The chain ferry *Duchess of York* can be seen on the foreshore, never to make the cross-harbour journey again.

Left: A lorry-load of hardcore embarks aboard the *Alexandra* for the journey from Portsmouth to Gosport.

36 Portchester Castle

Portchester Castle, positioned at the upper reaches of the harbour, is a structure which stands on a peninsula used by man for thousands of years.

To the north the great ridge of land, Portsdown Hill, shelters the area from the sharp northerly winds, providing Portchester with a more equable climate than some other parts of the coast.

The castle started life as a Roman fortress, and was built to withstand any attack. The walls were about 20 ft. in height, 12 ft. thick at the base, and were built of alternate layers of flint and mortar, bonded by tiles and limestone slabs. It has been estimated that 24,000 cubic yards of material was used, most of which had to be laboriously carried to the site. However much of the lime was obtained locally from the Portchester chalk pit half-way up the present Hill Road.

Now the ancient castle is in retirement, and is a place of recreation and relaxation. It hosts various historical pageants, illustrating in some small way the tumultuous ages throughout which the castle has existed.

Facing page: The Gosport shoreline makes a backdrop for this unusual view of Portchester Castle in the days when the trees still stood in the castle grounds.

Left: Portchester Castle between the wars, showing the custodian's quarters near the land gate. This old wooden building has since been removed.

37 Cams Hill, Fareham

A strangely deserted Cams Hill and Southampton Road at Fareham is evident in this 1956 picture. Thick trees line the northern side of the road, which today consists of residential properties.

The building in the foreground is Fareham Girls' Grammar School, now a mixed Cams Hill School. The building was just nearing completion and was officially opened in the following year by the Bishop of Portsmouth. The school was built on part of the North Park of Cams Hall, a stately home built in the late 18th century. The opulent building was designed by Jacob Leroux for the Delme family, especially for Lady Betty Delme, who prevailed upon her husband to move from Place House at Titchfield, to be nearer to the commerce and bustle of Portsmouth.

The new house became so expensive to build that Place House was cannibalised to provide building materials for Cams. The staircases, oak beams, and panelling were all taken from the medieval palace and brought to Fareham, and even the richly-carved oak supports from the Place House chapel were removed and used in the stables at Cams.

Cams Hall now is part of a golf club.

Facing page: North Park and Cams Hill. Top left, in the background and almost surrounded by trees, is one of Palmerston's Follies – Fort Wallington. The fort faced outwards – to beat a landward invasion – and it is a credit to the design that it is all but invisible when approaching from the north.

Left: Cams Hall in the '50s gradually becoming derelict.

38 Portsmouth Harbour

A helicopter hovers over the northern reaches of Portsmouth harbour in this unusual picture from 1956, from which we are reminded of how much the area has changed over the last 40 years.

The twin chimneys of the Portsmouth Power Station have now disappeared, to be replaced by a housing estate. The power station itself replaced older homes, one of which was the Highbury Street house of crippled Portsmouth cobbler John Pounds, who was instrumental in forming the Ragged Schools movement, when education was something that only the wealthy could afford.

The skyline of Gosport is also totally different to that of today. Then the only buildings with enough height to notice were the submarine escape training tower at HMS *Dolphin*, and Holy Trinity Church.

Now the harbour tower blocks, built in the '70s, dominate the horizon.

With the Cold War always threatening, there were more ships moored at the top of the harbour than today, and a couple more ships of the line can be seen in the Solent.

Between the anchored vessels in the middle of the picture there is a curious structure with four high pillars, which looks supiciously like a Mulberry harbour pierhead with its 'spud' legs in the 'raised' position, a left-over from the D-Day invasion.

Facing page: The helicopter pilot gets a bird's-eye-view of the northern reaches of Portsmouth harbour.

Left: Always busy; the harbour at the turn of the century.

39   Old Portsmouth

The huge shape of the 30,000-ton aircraft carrier HMS *Victorious* moves past Old Portsmouth and the historic Round Tower on her way to several months' sea trials following a seven-year rebuilding programme in the dockyard.

Hundreds of well-wishers stationed themselves by the Hot Walls and Sally Port to see the departure on 3 February 1958, and for hours Old Portsmouth was clogged with cars and cycles. Her departure was a real naval occasion, and completely overshadowed that of the Royal Yacht *Britannia*, which preceded the carrier out of harbour by 10 minutes.

Two helicopters were on the forward part of *Victorious*'s flight-deck, and another aircraft was stationed on the after deck. Such was the occasion that the sky was streaked with the vapour trails of aircraft circling the Portsmouth area.

The flight-deck was lined – as is customary – by the ship's company, but an unusual sight was a fairly large contingent of dockyard civilian technicians who were to accompany *Victorious* throughout her sea trials.

The ocean-going tug *Capable* was standing by, but the huge vessel made her way out to Spithead under her own power.

Facing page: *Victorious*, her deck letter standing out near her stern, eases past the Old Portsmouth fortifications, with the huge bulk of the power station in the background.

Left: Portsmouth Navy Days give civilians the opportunity to see the ships, and here a small group is being shown around the destroyer HMS *Zephyr*.

40 Clarence Parade, Southsea

It is the 1958 August Bank Holiday weekend at Southsea, and cars and coaches are building up on the parking area near Clarence Pier.

Visitors were given a wide choice of entertainment: Cowes Week had an ever-changing panorama of yachts on the move in the Solent, while at the dockyard the annual Navy Days offered the opportunity to 'see the ships and meet the men.'

Sunseekers would have found warm spots near the hot walls at Old Portsmouth, while both piers offered entertainment of differing kinds.

The fairground at Clarence Pier was advertising a special offer of five 6d. tickets for 2s., while at South Parade Pier there was a fishing tournament.

In the evenings there was enough variety for everyone. At South Parade Pier veteran comedian Arthur Askey was starring with comedy duo Mike and Bernie Winters, while at the Kings Theatre TV magician David Nixon was entertaining with singer Joan Regan.

And if you were pop minded, the group Manfred Mann could be seen at the *Railway Hotel*, Fratton.

Facing page: Private cars and coaches start to fill the car park near Clarence Pier.

Below: Queues await transport home after a day at Southsea on a warm Bank Holiday.

41 Victoria Barracks, Portsmouth

The complex of Victoria, Cambridge, and Clarence Barracks was commenced in 1880, and was built using convict labour.

The unfortunate prisoners were marched under guard from the Portsea prison, and such was the pity shown them by residents that little packets of sweets and tobacco were dropped for them as they passed. One convict, who worked on the heraldic carvings on the main building, asked to stay on after his sentence had expired to complete the work.

Victoria Barracks were occupied by a regiment of the King's Own Scottish Borderers until 1939. After the war – during which the tower suffered a drastic hit – the barracks were passed to the Royal Navy.

Clarence Barracks, now the city museum and art gallery in what is now Museum Road, was occupied by Wrens during the Second World War. The front of the building, which is very reminiscent of a French chateau with its stylised towers, is out of public view, as the museum main entrance is now situated in the less interesting rear of the building.

Much of the complex was demolished in 1967, and workmen discovered a thick wall, thought to be part of the old moat defences. A large amount of the area is now occupied by the Pembroke Park housing development and a hotel.

Facing page: The barracks complex before the demolition process commenced.

Left: Clarence Barracks during the Wrens' occupation. Note the French-style towers.

42 Portsmouth Harbour

At 10 a.m. on 4 August 1960, the mighty 44,000-ton *Vanguard* left the dockyard on her last voyage – to the breaker's yard. She was being towed out of the harbour, watched by hundreds of spectators, many of whom had travelled to Portsmouth specially to pay their last respects.

Suddenly the great ship – 814 ft. in length – veered towards Gosport, corrected her swing, and then turned towards Old Portsmouth where she ran aground on a mud bank near the *Still and West* public house. She towered over the floating bridge, sparking fears that she would damage the driving chains. She was refloated after about an hour with the help of a brace of Spithead tugs, and resumed her journey.

The *Vanguard* was laid down at Clydebank in 1941 and was commissioned in 1946, and at the time was the largest warship in the UK. In 1947 she made news by carrying the Royal Family to South Africa, on the first visit to that country by a reigning monarch and his queen.

However *Vanguard* was not the first ship to go aground in the harbour. On 12 January 1934, HMS *Nelson*, the flagship of Admiral Sir William Boyle, Commander in Chief of the Home Fleet, was aground for most of the day. In a highly imaginative attempt to refloat her, the ammunition was unshipped, and the full complement of more than 1,000 ratings were assembled on the stern deck and were ordered to jump up and down, while two destroyers sped around, creating a wash.

Although the Nelson finally got under way again, the ships had caused such a swell that the bow of the floating bridge was submerged, and lifting gear had to be brought in to right her.

Facing page: This superb picture by *Evening News* photographer Roy West shows the huge bow of the *Vanguard* dwarfing the spectators at Old Portsmouth.

Left: The royal party is welcomed at Portsmouth upon the return from South Africa aboard *Vanguard*.

43   Havant

The Market Parade development, when it was bright and new, is seen on this picture from 1963. The parade is still in operation, although the area to the right is taken up by the Meridian Centre, the new shopping complex in the town centre.

The railway station, to the left of the photograph, is basically the third to stand on the site. The first was constructed in the 1860s, and it went through extensive modernisation in 1889. The present station building was built in 1938.

The line to Havant from Godalming was built by speculative builders in 1858, and was leased to the London and South Western Railway. The London, Brighton and South Coast Railway was already running along the coast from Brighton to Portsmouth. To provide a through service from London to Portsmouth the LSWR had to run over LBSCR track from Havant to Port Creek.

In December 1858 LBSCR employees removed part of the track and blocked the line with an engine to prevent LSWR trains from entering Havant. The local press, never letting the facts get in the way of a good story, gave the subsequent altercation the fanciful name of the Battle of Havant, and intimated that a number of protagonists were involved.

In reality one employee had his shirt torn – but such is the power of the press!

Facing page: The holiday island-bound Hayling Billy waits to depart from the right of the main platform.

Left: An evocative view of Havant town centre in those days when traffic was far less dense.

44 Havant Bypass

The bypass around Havant starts to eat its way into the surrounding fields in 1964. Park Road South runs up through the picture from the bottom left, passing the large detached building which was the former Havant Grammar School.

In the centre is Bosmere Middle School, now completely rebuilt, and standing at the edge of the flyover which carries the A27 over the road to Hayling. The fields opposite the school, on the west side of Park Road, are now occupied by factories and offices.

Park Road continues out of the picture at the bottom left as Langstone Road, where it crosses the bridge into Hayling.

South Street, Havant, can be seen running down from St Faith's Church and curving back westward to join Langstone Road. It is now a cul-de-sac.

Facing page: The chalk mountain begins to build up around south Havant as the bypass nears completion.

Left: East Street, Havant, just after the turn of the century.

45 Hilsea, Portsmouth

The A27 – part of the trunk road system carrying traffic from the Channel ports to the West Country holiday areas – runs parallel to the Hilsea moat.

With the opening of Highbury College on 17 September 1963, and the growth of the Highbury estate, a route across the creek was needed to carry pedestrian and cycle traffic into and out of the city, avoiding the new, and very busy, Hilsea roundabout.

From the bridge there is an almost continuous view of Portsdown Hill, from the long slope at Down End, near Fareham, to Bedhampton in the east.

Today the bridge crosses the creek and ten lanes of highway, showing how foresight has paid off.

Facing page: The Territorial Army centre stands near the foot of the long curve of the bridge at Highbury.

Below: The Highbury estate during the early days of construction. This is Chatworth Avenue with some of the debris of the building site still apparent.

46 Wallington roundabout, Fareham

The roundabout at Fareham quay looks very different today as the flyover runs parallel with the railway viaduct. The impressive 17-arch structure was built in 1848 when the railway came to the town.

Over the years Fareham quay was a thriving enterprise. In medieval times it was a free port, with much business being done from the shipping of wine and the repair and building of ships.

Timber was exported, hides from the tannery at Wallington, and pottery and bricks from the local fields. The brickmaking industry finally ceased in the '70s, but the distinctive white-banded chimney pots can widely be seen as a permanent reminder.

The area also supported a tide mill, which was demolished just after the First World War.

Thackeray, who spent his school holidays at Fareham, called it 'a dear little old Hampshire town'. The town has grown apace since his time, but High Street, with its fine Georgian buildings, is virtually unchanged.

Facing page: The long line of the viaduct bisects this picture of the roundabout at Wallington. There is quite a build-up of traffic at the roundabout, although the number of vehicles would look small compared with that of today.

Left: The viaduct dominates this evocative picture from 1938, when life was slower and cars were fewer.

47 Charlotte Street, Portsmouth

The grey concrete swirls of the Tricorn complex dominate this picture of the central area of Portsmouth, most of which today has been developed into The Cascades shopping centre.

A vestige of the Charlotte Street market is still visible, although it lacks the scale and importance of earlier years.

The Tricorn was first planned in 1962 and work started soon after on the unconventional award-winning design that was to incorporate the existing fruit and vegetable market into the development, along with a supermarket, shops, car parking, and residential flats.

The scheme was set to cost £15 million, but even while the building was still progressing the design, using tons of natural concrete, was already being criticised. At that time its unofficial name was 'the Casbah' because of the eastern look to the towers that were raised first. In the building more than 30,000 cubic yards of concrete was used.

The fruit market started operations in May 1966, and the rest of the complex was to be in use within a year. However the shops never materialised as was hoped, the supermarket only remained open for a few years, and soon the huge grey complex was dubbed the city's white elephant. To add to the problems it was voted the country's ugliest building.

Facing page: The central area of Portsmouth showing the area that is now the Cascades shopping centre. North of Commercial Road, where the cars are parked, now stands the Tesco store and the National Car Parks multi-storey parking building.

Left: The Charlotte Street market in the early post-war days when bargains could still be had.

48   Guildhall Square, Portsmouth

Even in the 1970s large areas of the city centre had never been redeveloped since the war so, when the city council decided to pedestrianise the Guildhall Square and build new civic offices, many of the small streets were never to be seen again.

The Theatre Royal still stands in what is now Guildhall Walk, but before the war it had a companion, sited almost opposite. The Hippodrome was one of a number built and owned by Sir Walter de Frece. It was constructed in 1907, and was designed by the celebrated theatre architect Bertie Crewe. It cost the staggering sum of £40,000, and boasted a grand tier and a gallery, and four boxes flanking the huge marble proscenium arch. The auditorium was decorated in crimson and gold.

The opening ceremony was performed by Marie Tempest before an audience of 1,000, which included Bertie Crewe and Lady de Frece – the music hall star Vesta Tilley.

From April 1933 the theatre was offering non-stop variety and films to try to cash in on the talkies craze. However this experiment was short-lived and the Hippodrome reverted to variety on week-days and films at the week-end.

Along with the Princes Theatre in Lake Road, which was destroyed in 1940, the city lost the Hippodrome in 1941 during the height of the Blitz, and the site is now an office block, appropriately named Hippodrome House.

The Blitz, however, left behind a dangerous legacy. In 1984, during the demolition of the old theatre, workers unearthed an unexploded 500lb bomb. The Guildhall Square area had to be evacuated, and entertainer Bob Hope, who was to have appeared at the Guildhall, arrived in the city to find his show cancelled.

Facing page: The Hippodrome site can be seen in the top left corner of this picture, showing the area being cleared for the huge city centre redevelopment plan.

Left: An ignominious finale to the Hippodrome, after the air raid which spelled its end.

49   Portsdown Park

The huge housing estate of Portsdown Park, built on the hill slopes where once Bank Holiday fairs were held, was intended to be the showcase of the city council's housing programme. Instead it was destined to become an embarrassment, and was demolished after a mere nine years.

The project was actually started in 1965 when the council offered a £1,000 prize for the winning design. Work began in May 1968 at a projected cost of £2.5 million. By 1973 the construction company had left the site, and a search was initiated to find a new contractor to complete the buildings and to undertake remedial work on water penetration of the existing homes.

By July 1975 the final dwellings were handed over to tenants, but the water penetration and condensation problems were still apparent, and residents handed in a list of complaints to the then MP for Portsmouth North, Frank Judd. According to the list, condensation ran down walls and dripped from light sockets; carpets became like wet sponges; and clothing left inside wardrobes became mouldy.

In addition they complained that there was no adequate bus service to the estate, rents were higher than elsewhere, and there were continuing problems with gangs of vandals. They described the estate as 'the most unpopular place to live in Hampshire'.

By 1976 the city council was told that the cost of remedial work and technical advice had amounted to £700,000, and by 1987 the council decided that enough was enough, and it was agreed that the whole estate should be demolished, and new high-quality homes for the private sector should be built.

Facing page: The lines of high-rise buildings on the ill-fated housing estate dominate the hill slopes.

Left: End of the road for the park, as a demolition company's bulldozer, lowered on to the roof by helicopter, gradually works its way down through the floor levels.

50 Southsea

The thoroughfare now known as Palmerston Road was originally one of the most ancient roads outside the town walls, and it formed, with the present-day Marmion Road and Fratton Road, the main highways of Fratton Manor.

Until 1800 it was bordered by farm land, with just a few thatched cottages. These buildings increased in number and eventually became known as 'Hope Village', a name which remained in common use until long after the cottages had given way in about 1850 to more substantial private residences and shops.

The naming of Palmerston Road is perhaps obvious, and Marmion Road was said to have been christened after the name of the residence of a Mr. J. Webb, who at one time owned much of the land in the area.

In later years Southsea became the main shopping area, dominated by an institution – Handleys' Corner.

The store opened in 1869, when George Handley started his drapery business. The store grew and expanded, and eventually George's three sons – Douglas, George, and Trevor – took the reins. Handleys prided themselves on selling everything, even to the extent of an aeroplane. In 1932 when the airport opened, the enthusiastic aviator could purchase a Redwing 2-seater for £650.

The store boasted a roof garden where shoppers could rest their weary legs, and take in the scenery of the Solent.

Now the store is part of the Debenhams empire, but to older residents the area will always be known as Handleys' Corner.

Facing page: The corner of Marmion Road and Palmerston Road before the redevelopment of part of Marmion Road. The huge triangular area in the centre of the picture is now a Waitrose food store and car park, although Thomas Ellis Owen's Friary – just visible – was retained.

Left: Rebuilding commencing in Palmerston Road after the disaster of the Blitz.

51 North Harbour, Portsmouth

Work is under way on the North Harbour junction of the M27. The giant chalk bund is being built up, upon which the network of roads will rest.

To the north is the huge area of land, later to be dubbed the 'Zuider Zee of Portsmouth', 150 acres of reclaimed land which was destined to be occupied by the UK headquarters of computer giant IBM.

A Dutch specialist firm was brought in to conduct the reclamation process. First an area was enclosed by an embankment where a system of drainage channels allowed the water to be pumped out. A cutter dredger and its pipeline then lowered the seabed, and, by pumping the silt into the new bund at a rate of 80 cubic metres an hour, it built up the polder in roughly eight months.

The area to be taken by the actual building was infilled with Portsdown chalk, which allowed the pile-driving to be completed successfully. The first phase of the huge £17 million complex was opened on 4 December 1976 by the Duke of Edinburgh who then was guest of honour at a champagne luncheon party for 350 guests.

Facing page: The huge chalk bund takes shape in preparation for the motorway junction at North Harbour.

Left: Construction workers are busy on the motorway.

52 Mile End, Portsmouth

The M275 swings its massive way into Mile End, where work is progressing on the roundabout construction.

At the foot of the picture, below the road out to Whale Island, is the gas holder of the Rudmore gasworks. The huge structure, together with the brick wall built to hide it from residents' homes, would be demolished as the redevelopment progressed.

Standing out alone near the chalk outline of the roundabout is the Church of St John the Baptist, Rudmore, presenting a vastly different view to onlookers. When the church was built it was mostly hidden behind housing, but now it can be seen from all sides.

It was built at the beginning of the First World War in a very simple and austere style. During the following war the roof of the nave was destroyed by fire, and it was not until 1951 that remedial work was undertaken.

By 1980 the church became redundant, and has now been tastefully converted into retirement apartments with a difference.

Facing page: The cluster of buildings at Rudmore wharf depicts a different age from that of the high-tech motorway.

Left: The *Ship and Castle* public house can be seen in the picture opposite, almost hidden among the wharf buildings.

53   Tipner, Portsmouth

The long line of the M275 cuts a scar across Tipner Lake, as work starts on the 340-ft. bridge section near Whale Island.

Because of the route – mostly over reclaimed land and water – it is probably one of the few motorways to go into the centre of a city with such a small loss of existing properties. The road was an important one for an island city which hitherto had been served by just two roads to the mainland.

The official opening took place on 11 March 1976, and the tape was cut by Councillor Freddie Emery-Wallis, before he boarded a 1919 Portsmouth Thornycroft open-topped bus to lead the stately procession over the new road.

In the event the traffic congestion at Mile End, where the motorway ended, became so great that some years later a flyover was added to bring the traffic nearer to the city centre.

In the picture the greyhound stadium is clearly visible, middle left, as is the Alexandra Park sports stadium, middle right. In the background Horsea Island can be seen with the long artificial lake used for torpedo training.

Facing page: The area to the north of the motorway today has been reclaimed, and the Port Solent marina, with its shops, homes, and cinema, occupies the land.

Left: Cycling at Alexandra Park between the wars.

54 Portsbridge, Portsmouth

The 'new' Portsbridge is dwarfed by the build-up of chalk as the M27 construction continues. The roundabout, now one of the busiest and most dangerous in the county, is carrying very light traffic compared with that of today.

To the left of the picture is the Hilsea Lido which was opened in 1935. The remaining part of the Hilsea Lines was landscaped with paths at different levels to afford views of the northern reaches of the harbour and Portchester Castle.

Beyond, to the west, is the land that in time would be reclaimed and converted into Port Solent, the marina and shops complex popular with residents and visiting yachtsmen.

Facing page: The wide open spaces of the harbour stretch away towards Portchester, soon to be changed with the arrival of the IBM complex.

Below: Sparse traffic on the newly-opened Portsbridge.

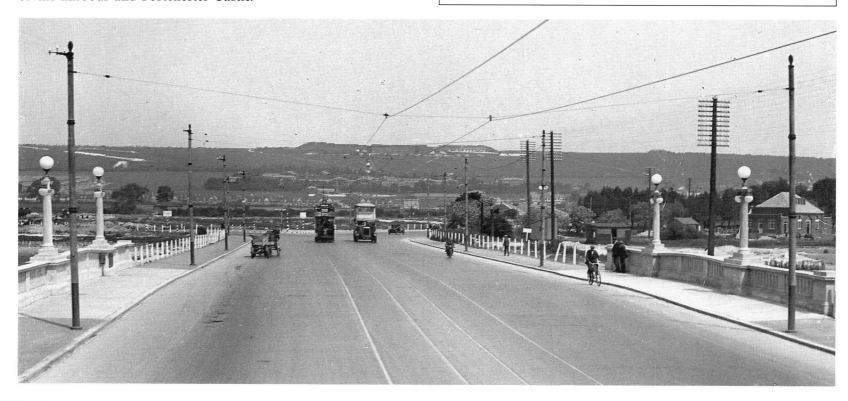

55 Somers Town, Portsmouth

The high-rise flats complex, dubbed the Gateway to Somers Town, stand high above an area which has changed beyond recognition during the huge city centre redevelopment.

Many old houses disappeared under the great plan to revamp a district that could no longer support the increasing population.

Small streets with names from the past were lost under the bulldozers, and in 1964 two cottages with original clay walls were revealed – a pair of buildings that could have been early farmhouses.

In the past Somers Town was gregarious, because most of its houses were tiny, and the people spilled out of them to gossip in the streets and in the public houses. But because the homes were so small, and insufficient by modern standards, the old Somers Town had to go.

The dispersal of the population to the new flats and maisonettes is not quite complete at the time of the picture – and there were still some streets of empty houses just awaiting the end.

Soon the teams will come and the area will be landscaped after the builders' huts and equipment is removed.

Facing page: Wilmcote House stands out on the building site that was to become the new Somers Town.

Left: The old Somers Road on a dreary wet day in the '30s.

56   Fareham

Work has started on the new-look town centre, which was to include a civic office-block worthy of the town.

Approval for the £31 million, five-year town programme was given in 1973, and construction commenced the following year, following plans which included a new health centre and covered shopping mall. The cost of the ten-storey office block was estimated at £2.5m.

In the beginning more than 6,000 cubic yards of soil was removed to make way for the foundations and, during the early stages of the work, special care was taken while driving the piles to avoid damage to nearby houses in the historic High Street.

From the roof of the 130-ft. building, councillors were able to see their previous home, Westbury Manor, down in West Street. The manor was to have been demolished, but after consultations the council decided to refurbish it and it is now the town museum.

The new office block was officially opened on 19 January 1977 by the then Lord Lieutenant of Hampshire, the Earl of Malmesbury.

Facing page: The white area of foundations stand out as the work is started. Westbury Manor can be seen top right, in West Street.

Left: The old buildings in High Street on a winter's day in the early '40s.

57   South Parade Pier

South Parade Pier started life in 1897 and was supposed to be fireproof. However in 1904 the unforeseen happened and the structure was all but destroyed.

By 1908 a magnificent new construction was opened which gave good service to the people of Portsmouth and for holidaymakers. In addition to the end-of-the-pier concert stage, it boasted its own theatre, which became the venue for many famous names, with concert parties in the summer and repertory and pantomime in the winter months. It originally seated 1,450 but, after alterations to the stage, this was reduced to 1,200 seats.

Many entertainers who went on to become household names started their careers in the end-of-the-pier shows, and many would have played at Southsea at one time or another. Although shows of this type were popular before the war, in the late '50s, with the advent of television, they began to close.

On 4 August 1974, during the shooting of the Ken Russell film *Tommy*, a fire broke out and damage estimated at £500,000 was done to the pier. However, like the phoenix rising from the ashes, the pier was rebuilt and is still a great attraction for visitors today.

Facing page: This stunning photograph from 1974 shows smoke belching from the burning pier as fire services battle to bring the blaze under control.

Left: The pier in the '50s, crowded during the summer season.

58 Guildhall Square, Portsmouth

The girders of Portsmouth's new civic offices rise from the huge area of land facing the historic Guildhall.

The £8.5 million building was set to become the most up-to-date office accommodation in Britain, and was designed to house 10 departments of the city council and its attendant staff of 1,100. Till then the various departments had been housed in offices and warehouses spread throughout Southsea, Old Portsmouth, and the central part of the city.

Staff began the big move, department by department, in July 1976, and continued until about September of the same year. The offices were officially opened in November 1976 by Earl Mountbatten of Burma, with all the pomp and circumstance that a naval city could bestow upon a naval hero.

Guests in the new building, and many hundreds in the square outside, watched the inspection of the band of the Royal Marines and four platoons of the Royal Naval Home Command. After the opening ceremony, hosted by the Lord Mayor of Portsmouth, Councillor Ian Gibson, Earl Mounbatten returned to the Guildhall Square to a fanfare of trumpets, followed by a rendering of 'Hearts of Oak' from the Marines musicians.

Facing page: An unusual view of the Guildhall in this picture showing the new civic offices taking shape.

Left: The former *Gladstone Hotel* at Southsea, for many years the council's main building.

59 Commercial Road, Portsmouth

A moment in history is captured in 1978 with the demolition of the old General Post Office, as part of the redevelopment of the city centre.

The Post Office as an organisation was constituted as a public service by a proclamation by Charles I in 1635. In 1637 the postmaster for Portsmouth was a William Brooks, and in 1660 the post was taken by innkeeper Robert Hophman, who petitioned Charles II for the position, saying he had been the only innkeeper in the town who had not taken up arms against the late king.

By 1673 a daily post journey between Portsmouth and London was established, although this was not done on a regular basis. The first mail coach was introduced in 1785, with the route taking in Petersfield, Haslemere, Guildford, and Kingston.

The General Post Office originally stood in St Thomas's Street, but in 1883 moved to what were considered to be palatial new buildings in Commercial Road.

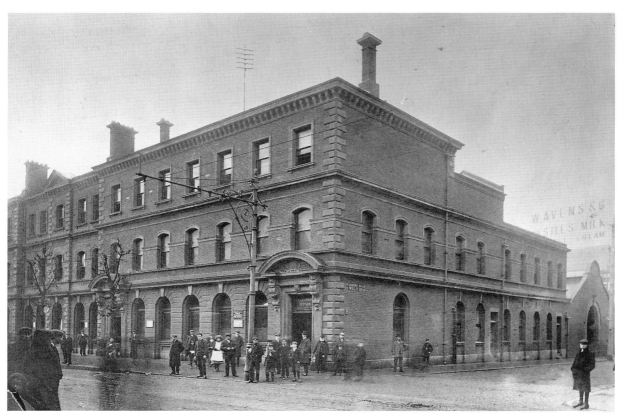

Facing page: The post office is reduced to a shell as the demolition teams get to work.

Left: Was it just the presence of a photographer that led this group to pose outside the post office in 1905?

60 Portsmouth Harbour

The huge iron-clad HMS *Warrior* makes a triumphant return to Portsmouth on 17 June 1987, after a seven-year refit to become one of the city heritage area's prime exhibits. She is accompanied by ships of all sizes, including a fire vessel whose hoses form a watery salute.

A special berth was built for *Warrior* at the Hard, where her masts tower 192 ft. above the waterline. In her day she was the world's most formidable warship, laid down in 1859 when Britain was looking fearfully at the French. She displaces 9,700 tons, with four-inch iron cladding over an 18-in. teak hull.

However her career turned out to be modest, for she never fired a shot in anger, and was paid off after a mere 23 years to form part of the floating torpedo school in Portsmouth Harbour, a role she held until 1924.

In 1929 she was towed to Milford Haven to become a floating jetty for oil tankers, and to all intents was left to rot. However, experts saw possibilities in the weed-encrusted hulk and she was taken to Hartlepool where a superb restoration process was undertaken, to bring her to her present condition.

Facing page: Smoke from a cannon salute at Fort Blockhouse at Gosport fills the air as *Warrior* is escorted to her new home.

Left: *Warrior*'s other historic companion in the heritage area, HMS *Victory*.

Bibliography

Allcock, G., *Gosport's Railway Era* (1975)

Barker, J., Brown R., and Greer, W., *The Cinemas of Portsmouth* (1981)

Brown, R., *The Story of Lee-on-the-Solent* (1982)

Burton, L. (ed.), *The Face of Gosport* (1988)

Burton, L. and Musselwhite, B., *Crossing the Harbour* (1987)

Caws, Sheila, *The Isle of Wight: A Pictorial History* (1989)

Cousins, R. and Rogers, P., *Bygone Havant* (1993)

Crouch, G., *The Story of Portchester* (1987)

Edelman, Ian, *Gosport: A Pictorial History* (1993)

Esmond, R., *The Charm of Old Portsmouth* (1958)

Holman, G., *Aerial Photography* (1969)

Howell, A., *The Topography of Portsmouth* (1913)

Mee, A., *The King's England: Hampshire with the Isle of Wight* (1939)

Mitchell, G. and Cobb, P., *Fort Nelson and the Portsdown Forts* (1987)

Mitchell, G., *Hilsea Lines and Portsbridge* (1988)

Mitchell, V. and Smith, K., *Branch Lines around Gosport* (1986)

Mitchell, V. and Smith, K., *Branch Lines to Hayling* (1984)

Moore, D., *Fort Gilkicker* (1988)

Moore, P., *Bygone Fareham* (1990)

Neasom, M., Cooper, M., and Robinson, D., *Pompey* (1984)

Offord, J., *Churches, Chapels and Places of Worship on Portsea Island* (1989)

Offord, J., *The Theatres of Portsmouth* (1983)

Riley, R.C., *The Growth of Southsea as a Naval Satellite and Victorian Resort* (Portsmouth Papers) (1972)

Robertson, K., *The Railways of Gosport* (1986)

Robertson, K., *The Southsea Railway* (1985)

Rogers, P. and Francis, D., *Bygone Portsmouth* (1994)

Robinson, D., *Giants in the Sky* (1973)

Stapleton, B. and Thomas, J., *The Portsmouth Region* (1989)

Triggs, A., *The Windmills of Hampshire* (1982)

Webb, J., Quail, S., Haskell, P., and Riley, R., *The Spirit of Portsmouth* (1989)

White, L., *The Story of Gosport* (1964)

Index

Picture Credits

The News, Portsmouth, frontispiece, 16, 20, 23, 24, 27, 28, 31, 33, 35, 37, 39, 40, 41, 43, 45, 47, 48, 49, 53, 54, 55, 59, 61, 63, 75, 79, 84, 85, 89, 91, 95, 97, 99, 103, 105, 106, 107, 108, 109, 111, 112, 113, 114, 115, 119, 123, 125, 129, 131

Hampshire County Library, Portsmouth, 13, 15 (both PFDP collection), 17 (McLaren album)

Lens of Sutton, 52

Portchester Social Club, 77

Portsmouth City Council, 10, 101, 117, 121, 127

HMS *Sultan* museum, 56, 57

BT Archives, 128